Spiritual

Intelligence

Dr. Amanda Goodson

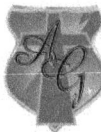

TM

Spiritual
Quick Books

ISBN-13: 978-0615649788

ISBN-10: 0615649785

Cover design by Steve Mason

Printed in the U.S.A.

Second Edition

Spiritual

Intelligence

Dr. Amanda Goodson

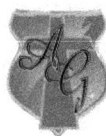

TM

Spiritual
Quick Books

Acknowledgements

I give all glory and honor to Almighty God for His grace and goodness. I am thankful for every life this book will touch.

I am grateful to the Never the Same Ministries teams across the United States. I appreciate all you do to seek the God's Kingdom and His righteousness.

I appreciate my family being patient and supportive of me and all I do.

FORWARD

Greetings Beloved,

It is with great pleasure that I write this forward for my dear friend and fellow laborer in the Gospel. Dr. Amanda Goodson is a 21st century preacher with wisdom beyond her years. The anointing on this book is designed to destroy and break yokes! After reading *Spiritual Intelligence*, you will have insight into the difference between normal intelligence, emotional intelligence, and the highest dimension of intelligence–spiritual intelligence confirmed by the anointing.

The book *Spiritual Intelligence* will empower this generation of believers with a greater anointing to help advance the Kingdom for Christ. This book will break the bonds of lack and bring the reader to a realm in the presence of the Almighty God.

It is time to change our "mind-set" and be people of intellect that only will be found in the presence of God.

Embracing His presence,

Dr. Laura M. Thompson

Table of Contents

Introduction

Hello! I am so glad you decided to join me on this journey to understand different dimensions and spheres of influence within the realm of intellectual capability as I share information on *Spiritual Intelligence.*

Every believer has the ability, power, and authority to advance God's Kingdom when used correctly (in the will of God). When motivated by the right motives, you will see consistent outcomes producing victory for the kingdom. In reaching this place, one will go beyond normal, emotional, and social intelligence to reach the higher achievement–what I call spiritual intelligence.

Normal intelligence is the ability to be educated, relate, retain knowledge, physical skill, and use that knowledge/skill in the earth realm to achieve/perform daily. Emotional intelligence is an internal knowing, and having insight into, what a person may be experiencing emotionally and what they may need in order to be more satisfied or happy. Mothers have excellent emotional intelligence. For instance, they can hear their babies cry and by the pitch of the cry, the mothers can know if the child needs to be fed, changed, or if they just need a nap. On the other hand, spiritual intelligence is the ability and skill to learn, understand and know how to move mountains, solve problems, and see in a realm outside the boundaries of education, emotion, and physical genius. This intelligence resides in the presence of God.

I visited the mountains in Arizona today and experienced a dimension of intelligence that I had never seen before. I heard the handiwork of God speaking to me in ways I had never experienced before. It was interesting to see people driving, cycling, hiking, and walking on the mountain enjoying themselves. Some of these people may never have taken a thought that that very mountain was crafted by God Himself for us to enjoy. I was in awe of the high peaks, the deep valleys, ridges, and the vastness of the mountains.

Exactly what do you think was on God's mind when He made the mountains, sea, sky, and the atmosphere? I believe when God created things, He had us on His mind to experience Him in unique ways. What about how we think? Do we think about producing great things for God by speaking them into existence like God did when He made the mountains? Do you ever think about that?

I have a lot of questions about how one produces thoughts. For instance, where exactly do thoughts come from? I believe a thought is simply an idea; a mental picture of a desired outcome, plan, design, or intention. I asked myself the question: Where does a thought originate? I believe all thoughts are words that live in the mind, and that words originated with Christ. Some thoughts get distorted, hindered, or twisted somewhere between heaven and the receiver translating the thought and acting on it.

I believe a move of God produces a thought. Our ability to catch the thought and move on it in God's will can be interesting and exciting for some. For others, they may miss it by paying attention to other things like a ballgame, a personal dilemma, work, or a fish fry. Your actions will depend on your level of obedience, understanding, the condition of your heart, and so on.

So, how does one create, capture, and expand on a thought? I believe we do it in the heavenly realm. This requires us to mentally transcend and evolve beyond the normal we see and reach a higher place in Him. Simply put: make God your top priority, dwell in His presence, and stay faithful to His Word.

What about intellect? Personal intellect is the creativity and ability to *know* something instead of *feeling* it. Relational

10

intelligence is the ability to relate well with others and the ability to sense when something is right or wrong. Personal intellect can come through book knowledge, common sense, through education, and training. Relational intellect is just a sense or insight about someone. However, spiritual intellect comes directly from God and His Word.

Through prompt obedience, careful study of the Word, prayer, and exercising Kingdom rights, there are so many successes that can come to fruition. With God, nothing is impossible. There is nothing too hard for Him–not even intellect.

Spiritual intellect involves and requires you to:

S – See Beyond the Normal
P – Place Your Thoughts in the Original
I – Intellect Goes Beyond What the Eye Can See
R – Realms of Intellect
I – Intentional Rotation
T – The Thoughts of God
U – Unfettered Access
A – Ambassadorship Versus Citizenship
L – Lessons from Successful Pioneers

I – Irrefutable Future
N – Next Realm, Please
T – Tell it from the Valley
E – Engineered to be Successful
L – Letting Go of Distorted Ideas
L – Living Out Your Dream
I – Impressions are Lasting
G – Go Grow Your Field
E – Expect God to Show You the Way
N – Now Unto Him Who is Able
C – Cadence of the Anointing
E – Everyone Can Have It

I trust you will enjoy reading these pages as much as I enjoyed listening to God while writing them. I have prayed that God will open your eyes to see how to be more impactful for His Kingdom through reading this Spiritual Quick Book™.

I have included at the close of each section several short exercises. These exercises are designed to help reinforce what you have just read, to help you apply the learning to your everyday life, and to help you become the authority in the Spirit realm that God purposed you to be before the foundation of the earth.

Live in your Kingdom with spiritual authority as a powerful person in Christ. Bear good fruit and make things happen in the mighty Name of Jesus our Lord!

1. See Beyond the Normal

After these things I looked, and behold, a door standing open in heaven. And the first voice which I heard was like a trumpet speaking with me, saying, "Come up here, and I will show you things which must take place after this."

Immediately I was in the Spirit; and behold, a throne set in heaven, and One sat on the throne. And He who sat there was like a jasper and a sardius stone in appearance; and there was a rainbow around the throne, in appearance like an emerald. Around the throne were twenty-four thrones, and on the thrones I saw twenty-four elders sitting, clothed in white robes; and they had crowns of gold on their heads. And from the throne proceeded lightnings, thunderings, and voices. Seven lamps of fire were burning before the throne, which are the seven Spirits of God.

Before the throne there was a sea of glass, like crystal. And in the midst of the throne, and around the throne, were four living creatures full of eyes in front and in back. The first living creature was like a lion, the second living creature like a calf, the third living creature had a face like a man, and the fourth living creature was like a flying eagle. The four living creatures, each having six wings, were full of eyes around and within. And they do not rest day or night, saying:

"Holy, holy, holy
Lord God Almighty,
Who was and is and is to come!"

Whenever the living creatures give glory and honor and
thanks to Him who sits on the throne, who lives forever and
ever, the twenty-four elders fall down before Him who sits on
the throne and worship Him who lives forever and ever, and
cast their crowns before the throne, saying:

"You are worthy, O Lord,
To receive glory and honor and power;
For You created all things,
And by Your will they exist and were created." (Revelation
4:1-11)

John was caught up to the throne room of heaven in this
passage of scripture.   John was invited to view a most
spectacular view of God's throne, the living creatures who give
thanks to God and sit around His throne and worship Him, the
twenty-four elders in white robes and gold crowns on their
heads, and the One who sits upon the throne. This spectacular
view of the throne of God is seen as a symbol of His
sovereignty, His rule and of His authority.

"And He who sat there was like a jasper and a sardius stone
in appearance; and there was a rainbow around the throne,
in appearance like an emerald." (v. 3)

Wow, what an awesome sight. The One on the throne was
called Holy, Lord God Almighty, who was, and is, and is to
come. They further stated that He is worthy to receive glory
and honor and power for He created all things, and by His will
they exist and were created.   From the throne proceeded
lightning, thunder, and voices, all representing the awesome
power of God. Seven lamps of fire were burning before the

14

throne, which are the seven Spirits of God and the fullness of the Holy Spirit (v. 5).

While John was documenting mentally, he said that he was in the spirit. He was not using his physical knowledge, intellect, or reason. He was just amazed at what he saw. John had to see beyond his normal physical means to see the glory, the presence of God, and the awesome views from heaven.

That is what we should do in our daily lives–see beyond the normal and what the natural eye can see, to then see what God would like for us to see. This requires a greater and deeper relationship with God, which will put you in a place 'see' through the physical or natural realm and into the spiritual realm.

It may seem strange because you are not relying on what you have been taught by people. Instead you are totally relying on God and His Word.

I was once asked to speak to a church group on the theme "Supernatural Jump from Faith to Faith, Achieving the Impossible." In preparing for this message, I started breaking down each Word so that I would know exactly what they meant. I asked God what He thought about the theme and scripture and how He wanted the message to be presented. The message revealed that to have a supernatural leap of faith that one must see everything that comes from God as a new normal. This requires us to see beyond what has been normal for us into a place in the spirit.

On the way to bible study that same night, realized I left my cell phone back in my office. I proceeded to go back to get it. When I went down the hall, I saw a gentleman that I had not seen in a while. When I first met him, he would talk to me in a silent whisper just like many are taught to talk in a public library. I asked him why he was whispering. And he said that

15

he had not talked in a very long time. He suffered a life-threatening event that required major surgery on his heart.

During all the surgical ordeal, something happened to his voice box. He was expected to die, but the doctors saved his life with an especially rare procedure. He was not disturbed at all that he had lost his voice during the event. He was quite pleased to still be living and to have the ability to see his wife and children daily.

A few months after that, I saw him again. I said good morning to him, and he answered, "Good morning," with a strong manly voice. I was astounded!! He could talk. I immediately asked him what happened and he replied, "I am not really sure. I just began talking one day." The man definitely believed in God (I asked) and His miracle working power. God had performed a miracle on this man, and he was a living testament to that fact.

John was called "upward" and was given the ability to see beyond the normal in order to get the Word to us and many others about God's magnificent throne room and about revelatory events. This gentleman was able to see beyond the normal and saw God's awesome healing power.

What about you? Are you willing to see past yourself, your circumstances, and your abilities in order to see God's awesomeness and routinely act on it?

Your thoughts:

In the space below, list additional reflections that you have in mind regarding God's purpose for your life right now. List what God has in mind for you over the next few years to see beyond the normal.

2. Place Your Thoughts in the Original

Seek the LORD while He may be found,
Call upon Him while He is near.
Let the wicked forsake his way,
And the unrighteous man his thoughts;
Let him return to the LORD,
And He will have mercy on him;
And to our God,
For He will abundantly pardon.

"For My thoughts are not your thoughts,
Nor are your ways My ways," says the LORD.
"For as the heavens are higher than the earth,
So are My ways higher than your ways,
And My thoughts than your thoughts.

"For as the rain comes down, and the snow from heaven,
And do not return there,
But water the earth,
And make it bring forth and bud,
That it may give seed to the sower
And bread to the eater,
So shall My word be that goes forth from My mouth;
It shall not return to Me void,
But it shall accomplish what I please,

And it shall prosper in the thing for which I sent it. (Isaiah 55:6-11)

Our daily lives are a compilation of many thoughts. Although we have thousands of thoughts in a minute, we can only think one at time. We can choose to think a good thought and produce good results, or we can choose to think a bad thought and produce a less desirable outcome.

It is guaranteed that thoughts will produce. Every thought will end up producing some kind of result. It may take a while for the manifestation of that thought to come to fruition, but we can be assured that it will produce.

God's thoughts produce; and God's Words produce. Every Word that proceeds from God will produce. That is scripture. God is not a man that He should lie. What He says will produce whatever He wants it to; and every Word that proceeds from His mouth will accomplish everything to which He intended.

I believe we have the ability to think like Christ. That is why we are given His mind (see 1 Corinthians 2:16). The Word of God has the ability to convey supernatural openings of our minds so that we are able to receive truth. Where our understanding was once dull, the Word allows us to now clearly see.

Our thoughts should always reflect the mind of Christ in every way. So when we speak, we will see the result that glorifies God in the earth realm. When we find ourselves drifting, we should repent, forgive self and others, and move forward thinking like Christ. We should move forward again speaking forth the Word of God, making things happen for Him.

In placing our thoughts in the original, we should go back to what God said about us in the beginning (see Genesis 1:28). We should strive to think just like the Word says.

God gave us an example of how a believer's thoughts will produce just like His did. Since we have the mind of Christ we should have His thoughts, intentions, and desires. Although we are not God Almighty, the Creator of heaven and earth, we were created in His image and likeness; therefore, our thoughts will produce the same that His produced.

We are His ambassadors and overseers of His creation. We should strive to think like Him. We should think like an original, place our thoughts on His Words and speak them forth. When we do that, we will need to use a different model of thinking; not of our own will, but of the will of God.

Your thoughts:

**In the space below, list additional reflections that you have
in mind regarding God's thoughts. List what God ways
you can think more like Christ–the original.**

3. Intellect Goes Beyond What the Eye Can See

Therefore we do not lose heart. Even though our outward man is perishing, yet the inward man is being renewed day by day. For our light affliction, which is but for a moment, is working for us a far more exceeding and eternal weight of glory, while we do not look at the things which are seen, but at the things which are not seen. For the things which are seen are temporary, but the things which are not seen are eternal. (2 Corinthians 4:16-18)

But what things were gain to me, these I have counted loss for Christ. Yet indeed I also count all things loss for the excellence of the knowledge of Christ Jesus my Lord, for whom I have suffered the loss of all things, and count them as rubbish, that I may gain Christ and be found in Him, not having my own righteousness, which is from the law, but that which is through faith in Christ, the righteousness which is from God by faith; that I may know Him and the power of His resurrection, and the fellowship of His sufferings, being conformed to His death, if, by any means, I may attain to the resurrection from the dead.

Not that I have already attained, or am already perfected; but I press on, that I may lay hold of that for which Christ Jesus has also laid hold of me. Brethren, I do not count myself to have apprehended; but one thing I do, forgetting those things which are behind and reaching forward to those things which are ahead, I press toward the goal for the prize of the upward call of God in Christ Jesus.

Therefore let us, as many as are mature, have this mind; and if in anything you think otherwise, God will reveal even this to you. Nevertheless, to the degree that we have already attained, let us walk by the same rule, let us be of the same mind.

Brethren, join in following my example, and note those who so walk, as you have us for a pattern. For many walk, of whom I have told you often, and now tell you even weeping, that they are the enemies of the cross of Christ: whose end is destruction, whose god is their belly, and whose glory is in their shame—who set their mind on earthly things. For our citizenship is in heaven, from which we also eagerly wait for the Savior, the Lord Jesus Christ, who will transform our lowly body that it may be conformed to His glorious body, according to the working by which He is able even to subdue all things to Himself. (Philippians 3:7-21)

I am assured that human intellect will not secure you a place in heaven. The only thing that will is your faith in Christ Jesus, with a true confession of the mouth and belief in the heart. Moreover, our faith in Christ requires knowing Him; but not just with an intellectual knowledge, but with an experiential knowledge and a shared life with Him.

Faith goes beyond what the eye can see–kind of the same as love in that regard. A lady at work asked me about faith one day. She asked me to explain it to her. I told her how I saw faith. I told her that faith was in the unseen realm and that it required her to go beyond what she knew and how she felt to a place where she could know. She quickly said, "Oh, I see, it is just like me being in love with my husband. I cannot see love, but I know I love him. I know it in my heart. He knows I love him beyond what he can see."

This kind of intellect goes beyond what you can see to a place of knowing. Spiritual intellect goes beyond book knowledge, physical endurance, common sense, musical ability, math skills, cognitive reasoning, and the like. Spiritual intellect allows us to make acquisitions from heaven and apply our requests to the earth realm. Spiritual intellect allows us to be fresh and flourish beyond what we see happening to the outward man–when gravity is pulling on our members (saggy skin, wrinkles, flabby muscles, etc.), it goes beyond physical achievement and emotional involvement to a place of knowing.

Spiritual intellect carries weight. As we mature in the Spirit, we come to a place of no worries because we know God will take care of our every need. We come to a place of knowing that God will provide for us according to His riches in glory. We are not troubled or anxious for anything; we just go to prayer and make our requests known to God. Then the peace that passes all understanding (a knowing) will be a guard to our hearts and minds in Christ Jesus, our Lord (see Philippians 4:6-7).

Spiritual intellect allows us to know and confidently meditate on things differently than a worrier, complainer, or confused person would.

Finally, brethren, whatever things are true, whatever things are noble, whatever things are just, whatever things are pure, whatever things are lovely, whatever things are of good report, if there is any virtue and if there is anything praiseworthy—meditate on these things. (Philippians 4:8)

Spiritual intellect knows the glory of being like Christ. He is our pattern for life. He never did anything against the will of

25

God. He showed us how to think, walk circumspectfully, and live a life pleasing to God.

Paul followed Jesus' pattern. He asked for us all to join him. Paul was sharing that our citizenship is in heaven. Going beyond what the eye can see, spiritual intellect will confirm (a knowing and security) that with our citizenship in heaven, our ambassadorship is on earth. Consider Philippians 3 again:

Brethren, join in following my example, and note those who so walk, as you have us for a pattern. For many walk, of whom I have told you often, and now tell you even weeping, that they are the enemies of the cross of Christ: whose end is destruction, whose god is their belly, and whose glory is in their shame—who set their mind on earthly things. For our citizenship is in heaven, from which we also eagerly wait for the Savior, the Lord Jesus Christ, who will transform our lowly body that it may be conformed to His glorious body, according to the working by which He is able even to subdue all things to Himself. (v 17-21)

Your thoughts:

In the space below, list additional reflections that you have about spiritual intellect as it pertains to you actually living in a place of knowing–beyond any human ability.

4. Realms of Intellect

For we are the circumcision, who worship God in the Spirit, rejoice in Christ Jesus, and have no confidence in the flesh, though I also might have confidence in the flesh. If anyone else thinks he may have confidence in the flesh, I more so: circumcised the eighth day, of the stock of Israel, of the tribe of Benjamin, a Hebrew of the Hebrews; concerning the law, a Pharisee; concerning zeal, persecuting the church; concerning the righteousness which is in the law, blameless.

But what things were gain to me, these I have counted loss for Christ. Yet indeed I also count all things loss for the excellence of the knowledge of Christ Jesus my Lord, for whom I have suffered the loss of all things, and count them as rubbish, that I may gain Christ and be found in Him, not having my own righteousness, which is from the law, but that which is through faith in Christ, the righteousness which is from God by faith; that I may know Him and the power of His resurrection, and the fellowship of His sufferings, being conformed to His death, if, by any means, I may attain to the resurrection from the dead.

Not that I have already attained, or am already perfected; but I press on, that I may lay hold of that for which Christ Jesus has also laid hold of me. Brethren, I do not count myself to have apprehended; but one thing I do, forgetting those things which are behind and reaching forward to those things which are ahead, I press toward the goal for the prize of the upward call of God in Christ Jesus.

Therefore let us, as many as are mature, have this mind; and if in anything you think otherwise, God will reveal even this to you. Nevertheless, to the degree that we have already attained, let us walk by the same rule, let us be of the same mind. (Philippians 3:3-16)

I beseech you therefore, brethren, by the mercies of God, that you present your bodies a living sacrifice, holy, acceptable to God, which is your reasonable service. And do not be conformed to this world, but be transformed by the renewing of your mind, that you may prove what is that good and acceptable and perfect will of God.

For I say, through the grace given to me, to everyone who is among you, not to think of himself more highly than he ought to think, but to think soberly, as God has dealt to each one a measure of faith. For as we have many members in one body, but all the members do not have the same function, so we, being many, are one body in Christ, and individually members of one another. Having then gifts differing according to the grace that is given to us, let us use them: if prophecy, let us prophesy in proportion to our faith; or ministry, let us use it in our ministering; he who teaches, in teaching; he who exhorts, in exhortation; he who gives, with liberality; he who leads, with diligence; he who shows mercy, with cheerfulness. (Romans 12:1-8)

This is such great scripture that shows the different realms of intellect. I would like to share about three realms of intellect; although you may think of others as you read this section. The first is natural intellect, the second is emotional or relational intellect, and last and most important, spiritual intellect.

As I mentioned in the introduction:

In reaching this spiritual maturity (intelligence), one will go beyond normal, emotional, and social intelligence to reach the higher achievement–what I call spiritual intelligence, or the anointing.

To reiterate, normal intelligence is the ability to be educated, relate, retain knowledge, to have a physical skill, and to be able to use that knowledge/skill in the earth realm to achieve/perform daily. This type of intelligence conforms and compares itself to the world's scheme, schematic, or design. This type of intelligence is learned in our schools today. Some of it is learned in seminars, lectures, online courses, and the like. It accommodates the world's systems of performance and has standards of what the world calls "normal, standard, excellent, intelligent, bright, and so forth." This type of intelligence will land you a prominent career path in business and industry if you have the right skills. This type of intelligence will tell you how smart you are according to the world's standards or norms. This type of intelligence will let others know that you pass with a certain grade point average, if you are magna cum laude, or the most thankful and humble, "thank you, laude."

Emotional or relational intelligence is an internal knowing and ability to have insight into what a person may be experiencing emotionally and what they may require in order to be more satisfied or happy. Most mothers have excellent emotional intelligence. For instance, a mother can hear her baby cry, and by the pitch of the cry, know if the child needs to be fed, diaper changed, or if they just need a nap. Relational intelligence is the type of intelligence a mother has when she looks into her child's eyes and just knows that they are not feeling well, that their feelings were hurt by someone, or that they just don't feel like talking today. This type of intelligence causes some to be deeply compassionate, emotional over circumstances, or angry over an injustice.

On the other hand, spiritual intelligence is the ability and skill to learn, understand and know how to move mountains, solve problems and see into a realm outside the boundaries of education, emotion, and physical genius. This intelligence resides in the presence of God. This is an anointing that puts you in a realm well above natural ability, literacy, bend, or education. This type of intellect cannot be learned in a school alone, but can only be taught by God. This kind of intellect can only be learned by hearing the Word of God, praying, fasting, and feasting on Jesus. This kind of intelligence is God's creative power working in you. It also will land you an excellent career in business and industry. With this type of intelligence, your motive will be toward "Kingdom building," not political or social status.

The spiritual realm of intellect knows that God is our heavenly Father, Jesus is Lord of our lives and the Holy Spirit is sent to us to counsel, guide, teach, reveal, seal, comfort, shape, and convict us. The spiritual intellect cannot be had or taught, but we are transformed to it. God began it, and He will finish it (see Philippians 1:6). This type of intellect knows that our image comes from God and that our original position is one of authority, dominion, and power. This type of intellect teaches us how to take off the old and put on the renewed mind (see Romans 12:1-3). Spiritual intelligence will cause you to change the atmosphere around you, release the gifts of God given to you, and bring heaven to earth through prayer and intercession on a consistent basis.

Paul cautions us to be careful of having confidence in the flesh, and that we should only put our confidence in Christ. He stated that he had a lot of accomplishments according to the world and religious standards. He had zeal and was righteous according to the law.

Although Paul gained all these things, he counted them nothing that he may know Christ in an excellent way. He further wanted to share in everything that Christ went through in his faith journey. Paul wanted to know the power of Christ's resurrection, the fellowship of His sufferings, be conformed to His death, and attain resurrection from the dead.

Paul knew that his spiritual intellect would allow him to lay hold of what Christ had for him. He pressed toward that goal. He knew he would continue to move toward that mark of the prize of the upward call of God in Christ Jesus.

He called for the mature to have the same mind,, not one enamored by the fleshly realm, nor one that is amazed by natural or worldly lusts, but by presenting oneself as a living sacrifice before God. He was asking us to give up everything that does not lead to Christ and give glory to God. He also, stated that moving in that direction would cause believers to not desire to be conformed to the pattern of the world, but instead be transformed by renewing of the thought life–the intellect. The type of transformation he was talking about occurs only as the Holy Spirit changes our thinking through the consistency of the Word.

With the spiritual intellect, one will know how to see themselves in relation to the word of God and the ways of God. We all can use our gifts accordingly in proportion to our faith.

Your thoughts:

In the space below, list additional reflections that you have in mind about the three realms of intellect I mentioned in this chapter. Where do you spend most of your time and energy? Please least five goals of how you can move from the natural to the spiritual realm.

5. Intentional Rotation

Then Joshua spoke to the LORD in the day when the LORD delivered up the Amorites before the children of Israel, and he said in the sight of Israel:

"Sun, stand still over Gibeon;
And Moon, in the Valley of Aijalon."
So the sun stood still,
And the moon stopped,
Till the people had revenge
Upon their enemies.

Is this not written in the Book of Jasher? So the sun stood still in the midst of heaven, and did not hasten to go down for about a whole day. And there has been no day like that, before it or after it, that the LORD heeded the voice of a man; for the LORD fought for Israel. (Joshua 10:12-14)

In my former career, I used to work with people who flew in space. I was amazed with so many stories that they shared with me about living and working in space.

There have been over one hundred space shuttle launches. As a space shuttle would fly, it would go into space at a speed of about 17,000 miles per hour to reach its orbit around the earth. When it is in orbit, it is on a different time than we have on

35

earth. It has a mission time that NASA would use to count the measure of time in orbit.

I have heard astronauts talk about the beautiful sun rises and sunsets when in orbit. We have one sunset and one sunrise daily. According to our time/calendar, in space they experience one sunrise and one sunset every ninety minutes. That fascinates me how God determined that way of doing things.

God had an intentional rotation and orbit for the earth, sun, and moon. He put them in to the heavens, He created the atmosphere around them, and can tell them when to start and stop whenever He ordains it to be so. Let's ask Hezekiah about it:

In those days Hezekiah was sick and near death. And Isaiah the prophet, the son of Amoz, went to him and said to him, "Thus says the LORD: 'Set your house in order, for you shall die and not live.'"

Then Hezekiah turned his face toward the wall, and prayed to the LORD, and said, "Remember now, O LORD, I pray, how I have walked before You in truth and with a loyal heart, and have done what is good in Your sight." And Hezekiah wept bitterly.

And the word of the LORD came to Isaiah, saying, "Go and tell Hezekiah, 'Thus says the LORD, the God of David your father: "I have heard your prayer, I have seen your tears; surely I will add to your days fifteen years. I will deliver you and this city from the hand of the king of Assyria, and I will defend this city."' And this is the sign to you from the LORD, that the LORD will do this thing which He has spoken: "Behold, I will bring the shadow on the sundial, which has gone down with the sun on the sundial of Ahaz, ten degrees backward." So the sun returned ten degrees on the dial by which it had gone down. (Isaiah 38:1-8)

God can start and stop time when He ordains it necessary. Joshua and Hezekiah have been witnesses to that truth. God also can make time move faster or slower according to man's understanding. Our astronauts are witnesses to that truth.

God has an intentional rotation of our planets. The earth orbits and rotates counterclockwise around the sun. Interesting, our orbit and rotation is intentional…it is around the Son.

Your thoughts:

In the space below, list additional reflections that you have in mind regarding God's intentional purpose for your life right now. List what God has in mind for you over the next few years.

6. The Thoughts of God

Thus says the LORD of hosts, the God of Israel, to all who were carried away captive, whom I have caused to be carried away from Jerusalem to Babylon:

Build houses and dwell in them; plant gardens and eat their fruit. Take wives and beget sons and daughters; and take wives for your sons and give your daughters to husbands, so that they may bear sons and daughters—that you may be increased there, and not diminished. And seek the peace of the city where I have caused you to be carried away captive, and pray to the LORD for it; for in its peace you will have peace. For thus says the LORD of hosts, the God of Israel: Do not let your prophets and your diviners who are in your midst deceive you, nor listen to your dreams which you cause to be dreamed. For they prophesy falsely to you in My name; I have not sent them, says the LORD.

For thus says the LORD: After seventy years are completed at Babylon, I will visit you and perform My good word toward you, and cause you to return to this place. For I know the thoughts that I think toward you, says the LORD, thoughts of peace and not of evil, to give you a future and a hope. Then you will call upon Me and go and pray to Me, and I will listen to you. And you will seek Me and find Me, when you search for Me with all your heart. I will be found by you, says the LORD, and I will bring you back from your captivity;

I will gather you from all the nations and from all the places where I have driven you, says the LORD, and I will bring you to the place from which I cause you to be carried away captive. (Jeremiah 29:4-14)

God has great plans and great thoughts about us. He is always busying Himself with thoughts about us. Sometimes in life, it may seem like the Lord has taken His eyes off of us; but that is not so. It may seem like He has not heard our prayers, but I believe as we live in Him, He hears. His thoughts are always to bring us back from captivity or bondage to our pasts, hurts, anger, bitter situations, sicknesses, or whatever may be in our paths that is out of alignment with Him. His thoughts are to gather us from whatever place or situation we find ourselves in, to a place of great success in Him.

God thought so much of us (loves us so much) that He gave up His Son, Jesus, for us. He gave us His creative potential and power to function like Him, to know Him and to make Him known. We can now rise above any circumstance and find our place in Him. We come to know Him in many ways like through nature, circumstances, the environment, reading, prayer, study of the Word, and more. There is not one area that God has left undone to teach us about Him. As we grow in His grace, we are able to search out the deep things of God in order to know Him better. We have His thoughts–we have the mind of Christ.

I was just reading Psalm 1 and got a renewed focus on the way of God's righteous people and the way of the ungodly. We are to be envied, happy, and successful because we follow God with our all.

Psalm 1

Blessed is the man
Who walks not in the counsel of the ungodly,

40

Nor stands in the path of sinners,
Nor sits in the seat of the scornful;

But his delight is in the law of the LORD,
And in His law he meditates day and night.

He shall be like a tree
Planted by the rivers of water,
That brings forth its fruit in its season,
Whose leaf also shall not wither;
And whatever he does shall prosper.

The ungodly are not so,
But are like the chaff which the wind drives away.

Therefore the ungodly shall not stand in the judgment,
Nor sinners in the congregation of the righteous.

For the LORD knows the way of the righteous,
But the way of the ungodly shall perish.

I named a life changing message I once taught "Do You Need to Change the Channel?" because sometimes we have growth opportunity areas in Christ. I call it changing the channel, because God sees the righteous as trees planted by rivers of waters where He streams information to us about His Word, purposes, intentions, will, and desires for us. God streams to us the great potential wrapped inside each of us to let others know how awesome He is. He streams to us so that we will not be like the wicked who are driven away by the wind. We can stand in the congregation of the called ones before God during the judgment with no sweat. When we line up and follow God, everything we do will be successful.

We are 'planted' by the rivers of water. Trees cannot plant themselves, and a person operating outside the stream of God is unable to transport him/herself into the abundance of God's

Kingdom. In order to appropriate the abundant resources of God which leads to productivity and increased spiritual intellect, grace has to be applied.

We are to be influenced by God's thoughts about us. We are not to be influenced by nor are we to allow others to shape our destiny. We are to get instruction and advice from the Word of God or from godly people (who God sends your way), we are to submit our thoughts and ways to God and do not hang out with sinners, we are to rest and relax in God. Meaning knowing He has got our back, our front, our middle, our beginning, and our end.

Let God stream (get information to you about His love, power, wisdom, and ways) to you. Meditate on His Word day and night. God is looking to unlock and release greatness in you. He promised Himself that. He is calling us to exercise our Kingdom privilege in knowing Him intimately. God wants to lead you to a great future. There may be bumps along the way, but nevertheless, God has a great plan for your life.

We are to pursue a course of action in life that points to Christ. We are to dwell and allow ourselves to be occupied with thoughts of Him. We are to be inhabited and consumed by His power. God wants us to turn toward Him every moment, and when we do, the results will be astounding.

That is how God thinks about us…He wants us all to prosper and have great success. His Word promises that we will be successful when we delight in the law of the Lord and meditate on it day and night. Sounds like a plan….those are God's thoughts about you. What do you think about Him?

Your thoughts:

How can you improve and spend more time enjoying, talking and meditating on God's word. What are you going to do differently to hear God? Also, make a list of what the word of God says that He thinks about you.

7. Unfettered Access

Then, behold, the veil of the temple was torn in two from top to bottom; and the earth quaked, and the rocks were split, and the graves were opened; and many bodies of the saints who had fallen asleep were raised; and coming out of the graves after His resurrection, they went into the holy city and appeared to many.

So when the centurion and those with him, who were guarding Jesus, saw the earthquake and the things that had happened, they feared greatly, saying, "Truly this was the Son of God!" (Matthew 27:51-54)

Unfettered access means no there are no restrictions or restraints in getting to God. Access is free through faith in Christ.

I was at this really huge facility last week that had security at the front desk that would sign people in to have access into the building. Some of the less busy buildings in the facility have front desks that close at 3:00 pm, and if a visitor has not checked at the front desk where they can retrieve their entry badge, they are denied access into the building. Employees have a special access key card to enter the building at their leisure, but as a security precaution, unbadged visitors are not allowed access inside of the building. The rule states that the employee is supposed to monitor the door until it closes shut so that people who are not supposed to be inside cannot get in. There must be a lot of secrets or secure work done in there (smile).

Anyway, one day an employee did not look behind themself and a family of three got into the building. The family did not know about the rules, but wanted some water because it was really hot outside. It turns out that extra security guards have the responsibility to ride around the premises of the building to make sure all is safe and secure. The family that got inside to get water without a badge was caught. The security guard came inside the building where they were and asked them politely what they were doing inside. The woman (with two small kids standing at her side) explained they only came in to get water and were waiting on her husband to come outside because this is where he worked. The security guard then asked her if she had air conditioning in her car. She replied, "Yes." He further asked her if her husband knew she was waiting. She replied, "Yes." He then told her that she could not stay inside the building, that it was a secured facility, and no one could have access without a badge. She immediately replied that she did not know that as she proceeded to finish filling her water bottle and went back outside.

The employee who did not monitor the door was apologetic about letting the unauthorized people into the building. There was no harm done; but the rules were just that–rules.

Jesus came and fulfilled every law identified by the Word of God. This does not mean that the rules go away. It simply means that we have access to God at any time through Jesus. We do not need a badge to get into God's presence. The tearing of the veil signified we all now have free access into the presence of God through a new and living way. We are no longer separated from Him. It was interesting when the centurion and those around Him finally recognized Jesus as truly the Son of God.

46

So when the centurion and those with him, who were guarding Jesus, saw the earthquake and the things that had happened, they feared greatly, saying, "Truly this was the Son of God!"

Many times I talk to people about asking God for anything and also the joy of being in His presence. When people are in trouble, I ask them to pray about what is troubling them. One gentleman said that he does not usually pray for himself, he prays for others because He did not want bother God with his little problems; he would rather God work on the problems that others have. I responded by asking him how he knew that God would not want to hear about him. I told him that I believe that God wanted to hear us all and can handle all of humanity's problems, whether small or great. God can even do it at the same time. He is God.

Another person said that they did not rely on God for the things that they could handle. I replied that God can handle it all, and that she should try God in every aspect and in every area in their life.

The veil in the temple was torn in two for us to seek God's presence and for Him to grant us access. You can go to God any time of the day or night. That is access.

Your thoughts:

Now that you have your ability to access God reaffirmed, what will you do differently when you are in the presence of God? What will you ask of Him?

8. Ambassadorship Versus Citizenship

Praying always with all prayer and supplication in the Spirit, being watchful to this end with all perseverance and supplication for all the saints—and for me, that utterance may be given to me, that I may open my mouth boldly to make known the mystery of the gospel, for which I am an ambassador in chains; that in it I may speak boldly, as I ought to speak. (Ephesians 6:18-20)

Brethren, join in following my example, and note those who so walk, as you have us for a pattern. For many walk, of whom I have told you often, and now tell you even weeping, that they are the enemies of the cross of Christ: whose end is destruction, whose god is their belly, and whose glory is in their shame—who set their mind on earthly things. For our citizenship is in heaven, from which we also eagerly wait for the Savior, the Lord Jesus Christ, who will transform our lowly body that it may be conformed to His glorious body, according to the working by which He is able even to subdue all things to Himself. (Philippians 3:17-21)

One of the most awesome things to know is that you are a citizen of heaven once you receive Jesus as your Lord and Savior. God already knew the decision you would make, but when you confess with your mouth and believe in your heart, you become a citizen. That means that all the rights, privileges, and benefits of citizenship are conferred upon you. Being a citizen also means you have fellowship with others like you and that you have the relationship with all believers as brothers and sisters. As a citizen, you have access to all that God has.

An ambassador is a person who has diplomatic rank as a representative of a legislative organization, government, king, sovereignty, or state. We are both citizens of heaven and God's ambassadors. Our citizenship attests to who we are and where we will live out eternity. Ambassadorship attests to whom we serve in our appointment or assignment on earth. Simply put, our citizenship says we belong and fellowship with God, and our ambassadorship shows we serve as God's representatives on earth.

I have met a few ambassadors in my life. Every time I meet a believer, I meet another of God's ambassadors. Paul walked in the call as God's ambassador. He knew that an ambassador stood as an official of high rank and authority for a legislative official. Paul was God's ambassador. He was identified by God for a specific mission and role. Paul was God's ambassador who was to shape the destiny of many people who would come to know Christ (that includes you and me).

I have read Kingdom leadership books by Myles Munroe and have heard his kingdom CDs countless times. In my learning I know that an ambassador is appointed by a king to represent the country or the king's interest, desires, and intentions. When you are an ambassador, you have every resource available to you to be successful. Also, you have all of God's wealth available to you, you are totally protected by God, you are embodied by God's interest, you possess diplomatic immunity, are to influence this earth for God, and you can never be recalled by anyone but God. Prayer and study of the God's Word will provide you instructions for daily living.

As God's ambassador and government agent, you are not defined by the space you occupy, but by the person you are purposed to be. You are to envision yourself as an ambassador appointed to an assignment, domain, or territory for Christ. Your power to influence and effect a domain is enhanced by your spiritual authority, spiritual intellect, relationships, obedience, faith, experiences, skills, gifts, training, education, and godly mentorship. Your authority to proceed (or succeed) is based on your assignment and purpose. You must see God's creative power daily at work in you because you are a participant of a greater mission which mandates you to add value to the greater good through your best efforts and contribution.

Jesus left us the greatest pattern for citizenship and ambassadorship. He was totally committed to obeying His Father's commands from heaven and executed God's Word on earth. Jesus was our example–we should obey God and execute exactly what He wants done on this earth just like Jesus did. Jesus even went farther for us. He knew we would walk in sin in this life and would need a perfect and sufficient sacrifice to be a citizen of heaven. He paid the price with His blood. As God's government official (by grace), I am grateful.

Paul followed that example. In fact, Paul encouraged believers to follow his example as he followed Christ. So follow Paul's example, speak boldly for Christ wherever you are. Speaking for Christ may mean that you are kinder in your delivery when dealing with a difficult situation. You may need to be more loving toward your neighbor. You may need to be more patient with a church member. You may just need to exercise self-control when going through a new challenge.

Your thoughts:

As God's ambassador, how might you execute the fruit of the spirit when dealing with a difficult situation with your home, church, workplace, or community? List 3-5 ways that you can represent the kingdom of heaven in a better way? Do you need to change your attitude or the way you see you brother/sister? Write your thoughts below.

9. Lessons From Successful Pioneers

Now Joshua the son of Nun sent out two men from Acacia Grove to spy secretly, saying, "Go, view the land, especially Jericho." So they went, and came to the house of a harlot named Rahab, and lodged there. And it was told the king of Jericho, saying, "Behold, men have come here tonight from the children of Israel to search out the country."

So the king of Jericho sent to Rahab, saying, "Bring out the men who have come to you, who have entered your house, for they have come to search out all the country."

Then the woman took the two men and hid them. So she said, "Yes, the men came to me, but I did not know where they were from. And it happened as the gate was being shut, when it was dark, that the men went out. Where the men went I do not know; pursue them quickly, for you may overtake them." (But she had brought them up to the roof and hidden them with the stalks of flax, which she had laid in order on the roof.) Then the men pursued them by the road to the Jordan, to the fords. And as soon as those who pursued them had gone out, they shut the gate.

Now before they lay down, she came up to them on the roof, and said to the men: "I know that the LORD has given you the land, that the terror of you has fallen on us, and that all the inhabitants of the land are fainthearted because of you. For we have heard how the LORD dried up the water of the Red Sea for you when you came out of Egypt, and what you did to the two kings of the Amorites who were on the other side of the Jordan, Sihon and Og, whom you utterly destroyed. And as soon as we heard these things, our hearts melted; neither did there remain any more courage in anyone because of you, for the LORD your God, He is God in heaven above and on earth beneath. Now therefore, I beg you, swear to me by the LORD, since I have shown you kindness, that you also will show kindness to my father's house, and give me a true token, and spare my father, my mother, my brothers, my sisters, and all that they have, and deliver our lives from death."

So the men answered her, "Our lives for yours, if none of you tell this business of ours. And it shall be, when the LORD has given us the land, that we will deal kindly and truly with you."

Then she let them down by a rope through the window, for her house was on the city wall; she dwelt on the wall. And she said to them, "Get to the mountain, lest the pursuers meet you. Hide there three days, until the pursuers have returned. Afterward you may go your way."

So the men said to her: "We will be blameless of this oath of yours which you have made us swear, unless, when we come into the land, you bind this line of scarlet cord in the window through which you let us down, and unless you bring your father, your mother, your brothers, and all your father's household to your own home. So it shall be that whoever goes outside the doors of your house into the street, his blood shall be on his own head, and we will be guiltless. And whoever is with you in the house, his blood shall be on our head if a hand is laid on him. And if you tell this business of *ours, then we will be free from your oath which you made us swear."*

Then she said, "According to your words, so be it." And she sent them away, and they departed. And she bound the scarlet cord in the window.

They departed and went to the mountain, and stayed there three days until the pursuers returned. The pursuers sought them all along the way, but did not find them. So the two men returned, descended from the mountain, and crossed over; and they came to Joshua the son of Nun, and told him all that had befallen them. And they said to Joshua, "Truly the LORD has delivered all the land into our hands, for indeed all the inhabitants of the country are fainthearted because of us." (Joshua 2:1-24)

Living in the desert longer than expected was no easy walk for Joshua after being held up for forty years before receiving God's Promised Land. After a word from God, all the desert living, the death of many men and women (a generation of people including Moses), Joshua was ready to move out. He sent two Israelites to scout the Promised Land and spy it out (Joshua asked them to spy out the land, especially Jericho), with the intent of godly takeover. Joshua was not playing around with this. Forty years ago, Joshua had this possibility under a great leader, Moses. But due to a lot of complaining and commotion from the doubters, God refused to send the Israelites to the Promised Land.

At this time in the scripture, Rahab a woman of Jericho who became a part of the linage David and Christ, then came on the scene to help out the spies. She told the spies that she knew that the Lord had given Israel the land and that Jericho was fainthearted because of the Israelites. After more conversation, Rahab had secured the future of her family, and the Israelites had what they needed for this new venture in God's will.

A pioneer is a person or group that originates and/or develops a new line of thought or action. This excellent team successfully created a totally new shift on the earth realm with their actions. Joshua, as a pioneer senior leader, developed a new way of thinking for Israel. Joshua shaped them so that they knew, through obedience, they would be able to move forward toward the promises of God. Joshua served as a great example of leadership for all to follow. Joshua waited on God for years; and after God spoke, Joshua moved. Joshua used the example of Moses, his leader to access God's presence and favor. Joshua used a capable team of leaders to go and execute the purpose of God for Israel, while he stayed with the home team to keep them motivated to serve God.

The two spies did not look for recognition on the way to executing their assignment given by their leader. They counted on the presence of God to lead them to the right place and the right people to achieve the results that would make the plan successful. The two spies utilized the resources available to them to make every action needed for Israel to work well. They spied out the town, got connected to a person who was willing to help them accomplish this assigned task, and they never compromised the plan of God in the process.

Rahab never knew what she was getting into as a pioneer leader. She made a choice. It seems to me that she exercised her faith in God to make things happen according to God's destined plan. She worked with the spies and helped to implement a plan for them to have what God intended. Her obedience to the requirements of the spies saved her family and saved her life. She provided an example of God's saving faith because she was clearly a woman who was at the bottom of the social ladder.

As a pioneer, she knew the right actions to take regardless of the circumstances and potential consequences. Her obedience landed her the right to be married into the family line of David and Jesus Christ Himself. By God's grace, Rahab became a part of the Messianic lineage.

God allowed these pioneers to be successful throughout their mission. He got the glory and the credit for the success…Let's take a look:

Now Jericho was securely shut up because of the children of Israel; none went out, and none came in. And the LORD said to Joshua: "See! I have given Jericho into your hand, its king, and the mighty men of valor. You shall march around the city, all you men of war; you shall go all around the city once. This you shall do six days. And seven priests shall bear seven trumpets of rams' horns before the ark. But the seventh day you shall march around the city seven times, and the priests shall blow the trumpets. It shall come to pass, when they make a long blast with the ram's horn, and when you hear the sound of the trumpet, that all the people shall shout with a great shout; then the wall of the city will fall down flat. And the people shall go up every man straight before him."

Then Joshua the son of Nun called the priests and said to them, "Take up the ark of the covenant, and let seven priests bear seven trumpets of rams' horns before the ark of the LORD." And he said to the people, "Proceed, and march around the city, and let him who is armed advance before the ark of the LORD."

So it was, when Joshua had spoken to the people, that the seven priests bearing the seven trumpets of rams' horns before the LORD advanced and blew the trumpets, and the ark of the covenant of the LORD followed them. The armed men went before the priests who blew the trumpets, and the rear guard came after the ark, while the priests continued blowing the trumpets. Now Joshua had commanded the people,

57

saying, "You shall not shout or make any noise with your voice, nor shall a word proceed out of your mouth, until the day I say to you, 'Shout!' Then you shall shout." So he had the ark of the LORD circle the city, going around it once. Then they came into the camp and lodged in the camp.

And Joshua rose early in the morning, and the priests took up the ark of the LORD. Then seven priests bearing seven trumpets of rams' horns before the ark of the LORD went on continually and blew with the trumpets. And the armed men went before them. But the rear guard came after the ark of the LORD, while the priests continued blowing the trumpets. And the second day they marched around the city once and returned to the camp. So they did six days.

But it came to pass on the seventh day that they rose early, about the dawning of the day, and marched around the city seven times in the same manner. On that day only they marched around the city seven times. And the seventh time it happened, when the priests blew the trumpets, that Joshua said to the people: "Shout, for the LORD has given you the city! Now the city shall be doomed by the LORD to destruction, it and all who are in it. Only Rahab the harlot shall live, she and all who are with her in the house, because she hid the messengers that we sent. And you, by all means abstain from the accursed things, lest you become accursed when you take of the accursed things, and make the camp of Israel a curse, and trouble it. But all the silver and gold, and vessels of bronze and iron, are consecrated to the LORD; they shall come into the treasury of the LORD."

So the people shouted when the priests blew the trumpets. And it happened when the people heard the sound of the trumpet, and the people shouted with a great shout, that the wall fell down flat. Then the people went up into the city, every man straight before him, and they took the city. And they utterly destroyed all that was in the city, both man and *woman, young and old, ox and sheep and donkey, with the edge of the sword.*

But Joshua had said to the two men who had spied out the country, "Go into the harlot's house, and from there bring out the woman and all that she has, as you swore to her." And the young men who had been spies went in and brought out Rahab, her father, her mother, her brothers, and all that she had. So they brought out all her relatives and left them outside the camp of Israel. But they burned the city and all that was in it with fire. Only the silver and gold, and the vessels of bronze and iron, they put into the treasury of the house of the LORD. And Joshua spared Rahab the harlot, her father's household, and all that she had. So she dwells in Israel to this day, because she hid the messengers whom Joshua sent to spy out Jericho. (Joshua 6:1-25)

Everything Joshua's spies set up worked. The same can be true for us, the Word of God will teach us everything we need to know about being a pioneer for Him. There are countless examples of those who have been forerunners before us and serve as examples to us. Abraham left his home country to be a pioneer, Ruth went with her mother-in-law to follow God; Hannah desired to have a son and went into the temple of God on her own behalf; Elisha was willing to follow Elijah before he was "taken up" for his mantle from God; Noah pioneered by building the first cruise ship; Mary pioneered by carrying the Anointed One; and Peter, Paul, and the disciples were pioneers for many Jews and Gentile Christians. What about you? What did God send you to pioneer or to assist with another's dream?

While following God's instructions carefully and accurately (marching around Jericho seven times), the Israelites were to shout in a high praise to the Lord. It may have seemed like a bizarre military strategy, but the people of God fully believed in God's promises.

So the people shouted when the priests blew the trumpets. And it happened when the people heard the sound of the trumpet, and the people shouted with a great shout, that the wall fell down flat. Then the people went up into the city, every man straight before him, and they took the city. And they utterly destroyed all that was in the city, both man and woman, young and old, ox and sheep and donkey, with the edge of the sword.

You can call anything to fall flat under the mighty hand of God! The scriptures remind us that there is nothing too hard for God for those who believe. Do you believe?

Yes, I know that nothing was to be taken from the camp and as we read further one of the Israelites disobeyed God, but that is another story.

This godly takeover was a great success! It went exactly according to God's plan. The gold, silver, and the vessels of bronze and iron were put into the treasury of the house of the Lord. Rahab and her father's household and all she had went with her. She lived with Israel because she hid the messenger leaders whom Joshua sent to spy out Jericho. These pioneers were prosperous in the Lord.

Your thoughts:

In the space below, what new ministry is God asking you to lead or to support? List the ways that you have seen pioneers successfully implement what was ordained by God in your church or community. What pioneers do you admire the most? Make a list.

10. Irrefutable Future

"Ho! Everyone who thirsts,
Come to the waters;
And you who have no money,
Come, buy and eat.
Yes, come, buy wine and milk
Without money and without price.
Why do you spend money for what is not bread,
And your wages for what does not satisfy?
Listen carefully to Me, and eat what is good,
And let your soul delight itself in abundance.
Incline your ear, and come to Me.
Hear, and your soul shall live;
And I will make an everlasting covenant with you—
The sure mercies of David.
Indeed I have given him as a witness to the people,
A leader and commander for the people.
Surely you shall call a nation you do not know,
And nations who do not know you shall run to you,
Because of the LORD your God,
And the Holy One of Israel;
For He has glorified you."

Seek the LORD while He may be found,
Call upon Him while He is near.
Let the wicked forsake his way,
And the unrighteous man his thoughts;

*Let him return to the L*ORD*,*
And He will have mercy on him;
And to our God,
For He will abundantly pardon.

"For My thoughts are not your thoughts,
*Nor are your ways My ways," says the L*ORD*.*
"For as the heavens are higher than the earth,
So are My ways higher than your ways,
And My thoughts than your thoughts."

"For as the rain comes down, and the snow from heaven,
And do not return there,
But water the earth,
And make it bring forth and bud,
That it may give seed to the sower
And bread to the eater,
So shall My word be that goes forth from My mouth;
It shall not return to Me void,
But it shall accomplish what I please,
And it shall prosper in the thing for which I sent it.

"For you shall go out with joy,
And be led out with peace;
The mountains and the hills
Shall break forth into singing before you,
And all the trees of the field shall clap their hands.
Instead of the thorn shall come up the cypress tree,
And instead of the brier shall come up the myrtle tree;
*And it shall be to the L*ORD *for a name,*
For an everlasting sign that shall not be cut off." (Isaiah 55)

After you read this section you should never doubt the provision, promise, and divine providence of God. As sinners, we have a way out of our circumstances to freely receive from God. Wow! What a God we serve. He is such an excellent

Father. This message to Israel is meaningful to us all today. This scripture invites us to feast on the Lord and His grace.

I know a lady who is what I call a budding Rose. She is so quiet and quick to help others. This scripture is so fitting for her right now. She needs to believe that God is there for her no matter what. When others persecute you and the enemy pursues you, there is nothing that God will not do to get you into His presence and to His provision.

She sometimes used to feel alone in life. Although she had family and friends around her, they did not quite understand her. She never tried to explain her position to others, yet she needed to believe she was a part of something big. She became a teacher in her church, and her life began to change. This rose began to blossom and reach higher places in Christ due to her commitment to the assignment.

Like the woman at the well, she knew there was something missing in her life. She was thirsty and hungry for something bigger and better in life. During her transition to teacher, she realized the importance of drinking from God's endless water supply. She realized that God wanted everyone to have this experience with Him routinely. We must realize that we have a need for Jesus in our lives and that He is the only way to be thoroughly complete.

What God has to offer cannot be bought with money; it is already purchased by Jesus. All that God has for us to be filled with His goodness is free. God's saving power is free. No one can tell you that they paid for God's saving power. But they can tell you that, at times, it was a rough road getting through.

This scripture urges the ungodly to seek the Lord quickly because we need Him as our vital necessity. Everything the Lord has spoken will come to pass just like the rain and the sunshine from heaven. No Word from the mouth of God will ever return without doing what God said it would do, and we will all dwell peacefully together with Him.

Rose learned that there is nothing that God would not do for her. She is learning to harvest what God promised her in order to prepare her for choice grain. She has the right priorities that will yield her a great reward. She understands that place and timing are important aspects of being in the will of God. Moreover, she knows that obedience will lead her to a greater relationship with God, and that her rewards are innumerable when she is in God's plan.

God is inviting us all to an excellent future. God invites us to a place of blessing that only can be given by Him.

Your thoughts:

In the space below, list ways you know your future is secure. God's word gives us assurance that He will honor His promises. Please put the scripture references with your list of answers.

11. Next Realm, Please

I am the LORD, your Holy One, The Creator of Israel, your King." Thus says the LORD, who makes a way in the sea And a path through the mighty waters, Who brings forth the chariot and horse, the army and the power (They shall lie down together, they shall not rise; They are extinguished, they are quenched like a wick): "Do not remember the former things, Nor consider the things of old. Behold, I will do a new thing, Now it shall spring forth; shall you not know it? I will even make a road in the wilderness and rivers in the desert. The beast of the field will honor Me, the jackals and the ostriches, because I give waters in the wilderness and rivers in the desert, to give drink to My people, My chosen. This people I have formed for Myself; they shall declare My praise. (Isaiah 43:15-21)

A realm is a domain or sphere of influence where a person is in charge. Of course for us, God gives the instructions. God went through great lengths to allow Israel to understand His majesty and awesome character and ways. He does the same for us. In this scripture, Isaiah is letting us know that God is our King and our Lord. Because of God's grace, the Lord will do many things for us.

In this scripture, God reminded Israel of who He was to them and that He and been there with them all along. There was nothing that happened in their past, present, or future that He did not know about. He further said that He made His chosen people for Himself, and that His chosen people will declare His praise. God was reminding the people that He had been their King from the beginning; and even though they had desired a human king (see 1 Samuel 8:4-7), they could still be restored through Christ the Messiah.

We should see God as our future Designer and Revealer. He seeks to protect our future in Him. We must leave the place of the past and of indecision. Right now is the time to see yourself moving into the next realm in Christ. In that realm, God will gather you into Himself, and then He will move you into a higher place with Him. He has many things prepared for you to have in another dimension than where you are. We must believe there is more for us to enjoy.

As you grow closer to God, you will discover how vast He is, and at that point, you will desire more. So many people live in the past. God is asking for us to enjoy the now and create a compelling future for ourselves and others in the next. This is done by doing things just like God did–speak them into existence. When you speak into your next realm, God will rebuild, move, plant, and bless anything you speak to in His will. Try it. God says He will do it for you, and God does not lie.

There are many facets to our next realm. In that place, you will be more filled with God's Spirit. You will seek His face more; you will ask God for the intellectual capacity to serve Him in a greater way; you will know that in every breath is the Holy Spirit and power; you will know that you are being prepared for greatness; and you will confidently know that what God began in you will be completed by Him.

So, go in to the next realm with confidence, and influence your future by what you say.

Your thoughts:

In the space below, list additional ways you can influence your next realm. Write a prayer to ask God to draw you closer to Him in a more excellent way. If Jesus said you could have anything what would that be? Make a list below.

12. Tell it from the Valley

O LORD, You induced me, and I was persuaded; You are stronger than I, and have prevailed. I am in derision daily; Everyone mocks me. For when I spoke, I cried out; I shouted, "Violence and plunder!" because the word of the LORD was made to me a reproach and a derision daily. Then I said, "I will not make mention of Him, nor speak anymore in His name." But His word was in my heart like a burning fire shut up in my bones; I was weary of holding it back, and I could not. For I heard many mocking: "Fear on every side!" "Report," they say, "and we will report it!" All my acquaintances watched for my stumbling, saying, "Perhaps he can be induced; then we will prevail against him, And we will take our revenge on him." But the LORD is with me as a mighty, awesome One.

Therefore my persecutors will stumble, and will not prevail. They will be greatly ashamed, for they will not prosper. Their everlasting confusion will never be forgotten. But, O LORD of hosts, You who test the righteous, and see the mind and heart, Let me see Your vengeance on them; For I have pleaded my cause before You. Sing to the LORD! Praise the LORD! For He has delivered the life of the poor from the hand of evildoers. (Jeremiah 20:7-13)

I used to live in a place called the "Tennessee Valley." Although I lived in Alabama, it was called the Tennessee

Valley because our state bordered several states, including Tennessee. The major waterway through our town was the Tennessee River. We lived in a valley; we were not in a high place. So, that is why we were called the "Tennessee Valley."

I never thought it about it much growing up. It did not seem too low of a place from my vantage point. It wasn't until I saw a different (higher) place, that I understood the valley.

Many of us have had valley experiences where we thought there was no way out. Jeremiah experienced several valley experiences as a prophet to Israel. So many times he was given a prophecy from God about doom and destruction of the nation. Well, the leaders and the people of that day did not like his message. He challenged the prophets who lied, he challenged world leaders who were acting inappropriately, and he also prophesied to the sinful condition of Judah.

Jeremiah also prophesied restoration to the people of God. He purchased land in preparation of being restored, he told God's people to build houses, have children and give their children in marriage–for the nation to stay vibrant and strong–expecting a good end.

In this scripture, Jeremiah had made a decision to not mention God's name to the people anymore. He was tired of being mocked and tired of being a reproach to the people. He prophesied about violence and plunder to the people of God. God had induced him and persuaded Jeremiah to speak those words. Jeremiah had a way to fix that!! He just would not speak about God at all–Jeremiah said that he would not even mention God's Name. He was in a valley. Just as he spoke the words about being in derision daily, he then remembered the Word of God was like fire that was shut up in his bones that would not let him be quiet about God. Jeremiah could not hold back.

Jeremiah remembered that God was a mighty, awesome God. God had promised Jeremiah that he was called from his mother's womb, and he was destined to be God's mouthpiece.

What about you? Has God asked you to do something profound for him but while you are having a valley experience, you have decided not to do it? Do you know of someone who reacted to their valley experience this way?

I submit that the Lord is awesome and He is vast. God is deep, He is high, He is wide, He is broad, and He is long. Nothing escapes God. Are you having a valley experience right now? Have you ever had one? Do you know of someone in a valley right now? Know that God will see you through. He is right there in that valley with you. Spiritual intellect impresses upon us to tell your story; even in the valley! So, tell your story when God wants you to. God will take care of you. He is the awesome One true God. Believe it!!

Your thoughts:

In the space below, reflect on a time when you had a valley experience and God brought you out. Write 5 affirmations about how He showed Himself strong on your behalf. Commit to honor God in all things. Write a sentence or two about your renewed commitment.

13. Engineered to be Successful

Blessed be the God and Father of our Lord Jesus Christ, who has blessed us with every spiritual blessing in the heavenly places in Christ, just as He chose us in Him before the foundation of the world, that we should be holy and without blame before Him in love, having predestined us to adoption as sons by Jesus Christ to Himself, according to the good pleasure of His will, to the praise of the glory of His grace, by which He made us accepted in the Beloved.

In Him we have redemption through His blood, the forgiveness of sins, according to the riches of His grace which He made to abound toward us in all wisdom and prudence, having made known to us the mystery of His will, according to His good pleasure which He purposed in Himself, that in the dispensation of the fullness of the times He might gather together in one all things in Christ, both which are in heaven and which are on earth—in Him. In Him also we have obtained an inheritance, being predestined according to the purpose of Him who works all things according to the counsel of His will, that we who first trusted in Christ should be to the praise of His glory.

In Him you also trusted, after you heard the word of truth, the gospel of your salvation; in whom also, having believed, you were sealed with the Holy Spirit of promise, who is the guarantee of our inheritance until the redemption of the purchased possession, to the praise of His glory. (Ephesians 1:3-14)

Engineers design, build, maintain, and operate things. They also have the ability to transform things into things that they were not supposed to be. They can take just a few items and create a machine, a widget, or gadget to solve any need imaginable.

So far in my lifetime, I have worked with countless engineers who have genius intellect in the natural realm. In this scripture, I see the creative geniuses God made us to be in the spiritual realm.

Through God's love, we are called and chosen to be in Him. He adopted us to be His very own before the foundation of the world. He architected and engineered us to function just like Him and accepted us in Christ.

Since we were architected and engineered before the foundation of the world by God, that means that we cannot be anything but successful when we follow His Word. This roll call of our successful future is absolutely amazing. Let's look at the list:

- We are blessed with all spiritual blessings in heavenly places (and on earth as an ambassador).
- He chose us in Him from the foundation of the world.
- We are chosen to be blameless before God in love.
- We are adopted as sons by Christ Himself according to the good pleasure of His will.
- We are acceptable to God like we are (He will continue to make us better and transform us daily).
- Christ bought us back through His shed blood.
- We have been forgiven of our sins (we should also forgive).

- We abound in wisdom, self-discipline, and right actions.
- We know the mystery of God's will according to His good pleasure.
- He will gather us all in Him.
- We have obtained an inheritance and have a pre-determined purpose according to the will of His counsel.
- We have a guarantee of salvation when we believe in Jesus (confession with our mouth and belief in our heart).
- We have the Holy Spirit as our seal of God's promise.
- We remain God's purchased possession and He gets all the praise, honor, and glory.

Your thoughts:

In the space below, list additional reflections that you have in mind regarding God's plan for your life right now. List what God has in mind for you over the next few years to see beyond the normal that points to your success in Him.

14. Letting Go of Distorted Ideas

For I want you to know what a great conflict I have for you and those in Laodicea, and for as many as have not seen my face in the flesh, that their hearts may be encouraged, being knit together in love, and attaining to all riches of the full assurance of understanding, to the knowledge of the mystery of God, both of the Father and of Christ, in whom are hidden all the treasures of wisdom and knowledge.

Now this I say lest anyone should deceive you with persuasive words. For though I am absent in the flesh, yet I am with you in spirit, rejoicing to see your good order and the steadfastness of your faith in Christ.

As you therefore have received Christ Jesus the Lord, so walk in Him, rooted and built up in Him and established in the faith, as you have been taught, abounding in it with thanksgiving.

Beware lest anyone cheat you through philosophy and empty deceit, according to the tradition of men, according to the basic principles of the world, and not according to Christ. For in Him dwells all the fullness of the Godhead bodily; and you are complete in Him, who is the head of all principality and power. (Colossians 2:1-10)

Every time I turn on the television, I see a commercial or infomercial that causes me to pause. I am encouraged that it is my decision to turn it off. I also have occasion to talk to people in the community about their ideas of how the economy is affecting our people or about pressing issues in the community. Inevitably during my conversations, I will hear someone talk about a philosopher and quote one of their sayings. At other times, I will notice one on an email at the end a quote from a famous philosopher or former president, official, or a famous person.

Sometimes, we do not realize what is influencing us. We do not know what and how things get in to our minds that cause us to react differently to others and to the Word of God.

We are taught to question things. We are taught to be creative and to come up with solutions to pressing problems. We are sometimes taught how to sit, stand in a room, and how to present a document to a team. We are told how and what to think to make it in this world.

The approach to learning and representing should be to point to Christ in everything. Although you may be required in school to learn other approaches, there is only one truth. Spiritual maturity grows and develops from the foundation of biblical truth. This rooting, building, and establishing is found in the sound doctrine of the Word.

In our society, our senses are stimulated in so many ways. Be aware of your surroundings, lift up Jesus in all you do. Look out for distorted words that may keep you off track.

Psalm 1 is a great example. About influence:

Blessed is the one who does not walk in step with the wicked or stand in the way that sinners take or sit in the company of mockers, but whose delight is in the law of the LORD, and who meditates on his law (word) day and night. That person is like a tree planted by streams of water, which yields its fruit in season and whose leaf does not wither—whatever they do prospers. Not so the wicked! They are like chaff that the wind blows away. Therefore the wicked will not stand in the judgment, nor sinners in the assembly of the righteous. For the LORD watches over the way of the righteous, but the way of the wicked leads to destruction. (Psalm 1:1-5)

God is looking to unlock and release creative power and potential in you. Distorted ideas will get in the way. Turn the channel and do amazing things for God's Kingdom.

God is streaming (sending us His Word, will, and way) to us as His agents on earth for us to be effective for Him. Because God is always streaming (speaking), we should delight in Him and meditate on His word. God will make us ready to bear excellent fruit in due season. We will be more successful and prosperous and have everything we need to do in order to fulfill God's purpose. In fact, following His instructions will cause everything you do to succeed.

The influence you allow on your life will determine your path in life. If you are influenced by empty talk, jokes, and conversation out of sync with the Word of God, your destiny will take a different turn. Therefore, do not follow the advice and plans of the ungodly. Do not be submissive and inactive by hanging out with sinners. Do not rest or get relaxed around the scornful or mockers.

God wants us to turn our attention toward Him in all we do. So, let go of distorted ideas and distractions in your life. The ungodly are like chaff which the wind drives away. God does little to no streaming to them. On the other hand, the righteous will always succeed. Follow God's instructions, you will be better and the wiser for it.

Your thoughts:

Have you ever been influenced by a distorted view of something? If so, then how did you overcome it? Are you hanging around with people who may not influence you in a godly way? In the space below develop a plan to get back to God and give Him first place in your life. How will you use your supernatural intellect to make this happen?

15. Living Out Your Dream

Now Joseph had a dream, and he told it to his brothers; and they hated him even more. So he said to them, "Please hear this dream which I have dreamed: There we were, binding sheaves in the field. Then behold, my sheaf arose and also stood upright; and indeed your sheaves stood all around and bowed down to my sheaf."

And his brothers said to him, "Shall you indeed reign over us? Or shall you indeed have dominion over us?" So they hated him even more for his dreams and for his words.

Then he dreamed still another dream and told it to his brothers, and said, "Look, I have dreamed another dream. And this time, the sun, the moon, and the eleven stars bowed down to me."

So he told it to his father and his brothers; and his father rebuked him and said to him, "What is this dream that you have dreamed? Shall your mother and I and your brothers indeed come to bow down to the earth before you?" And his brothers envied him, but his father kept the matter in mind. (Genesis 37:5-11)

I used to think that everybody had a dream, but that is not true. Some people just have a vivid imagination and cannot make their thoughts come to fruition. That is certainly not you.

God will give you dreams and desires to accomplish great things. It will seem unusual to many people, but hold on to it. I find that sometimes our dreams, can be mixed wrong motives due to lack of maturity in our faith and knowledge of God. So, don't let go of that BIG dream for greatness. It may have come from God after all, and He is waiting for you to mature to launch it in the correct way.

I know a lady who started her own consulting and speaking business in the early 1990's. She was gung ho about it, and nothing could stop her. She had spent a lot of her money on that dream by developing a strategy for success. She started with getting a sure strategy, developed goals, and a tactical execution plan. She had a team of people on board to help her. She knew that within a few months that she was going to be rich!!

She began to execute to her plan and things worked pretty well at first, but after time and lots of money, her strategy did not work. So, she turned away from her dream, she dissolved her corporation, and then threw away all of the documentation and information that she had acquired and written during that time.

She had spent time writing four books, had publications about her business, CDs, videos, and the like. She had a marketing strategy, she had her name in many businesses across her community and in many other places. It seemed no one was interested in paying her for her skills, but they offered to have her come consult and speak for free.

Her plan was to get paid for her services, and quit work soon. So consulting and speaking for free would not work. She had several more setbacks after that time, but to her credit, she never quit her primary job and she did not totally give up. She decided that everything was to be thrown away and she was to forget her dreams. She decided to concentrate more on church and Jesus.

After a few long years, God put in her spirit to write again and she did. This time, she wrote books about God and His awesome power to change people's lives. She was so excited, she was writing for God and being asked to speak.

This time, she did not mind volunteering her time. She only had to volunteer for a short while before others wanted to seed into her life for her gift.

Today, she has a renewed energy that is focused on God first. Since that time, she has been asked to write more books for industry and business, in addition to her faith based books. She is asked to speak in a few places the United States in conferences as a keynote speaker. She wants to contribute to God's Kingdom and honor Him.

With her focus on God, her dreams from long ago are finally coming to pass. Do not give up on your dream; instead, give up on doing it your way and stick to God's way. Live out the dream that God put inside of you!!

Your thoughts:

In the space below, list additional reflections that you have in mind about the dreams and desires you have had since you were younger. Make a list of what you intend to do in life for God. Make sure it is focused on God first.

16. Impressions are Lasting

There was a relative of Naomi's husband, a man of great wealth, of the family of Elimelech. His name was Boaz. So Ruth the Moabitess said to Naomi, "Please let me go to the field, and glean heads of grain after him in whose sight I may find favor."

And she said to her, "Go, my daughter."

Then she left, and went and gleaned in the field after the reapers. And she happened to come to the part of the field belonging to Boaz, who was of the family of Elimelech.

Now behold, Boaz came from Bethlehem, and said to the reapers, "The LORD be with you!"

And they answered him, "The LORD bless you!"

Then Boaz said to his servant who was in charge of the reapers, "Whose young woman is this?"

So the servant who was in charge of the reapers answered and said, "It is the young Moabite woman who came back with Naomi from the country of Moab. And she said, 'Please let me glean and gather after the reapers among the sheaves.' So she came and has continued from morning until now, though she rested a little in the house."

Then Boaz said to Ruth, "You will listen, my daughter, will you not? Do not go to glean in another field, nor go from here, but stay close by my young women. Let your eyes be on the field which they reap, and go after them. Have I not commanded the young men not to touch you? And when you are thirsty, go to the vessels and drink from what the young men have drawn."

So she fell on her face, bowed down to the ground, and said to him, "Why have I found favor in your eyes, that you should take notice of me, since I am a foreigner?"

And Boaz answered and said to her, "It has been fully reported to me, all that you have done for your mother-in-law since the death of your husband, and how you have left your father and your mother and the land of your birth, and have come to a people whom you did not know before. The LORD repay your work, and a full reward be given you by the LORD God of Israel, under whose wings you have come for refuge."

Then she said, "Let me find favor in your sight, my lord; for you have comforted me, and have spoken kindly to your maidservant, though I am not like one of your maidservants."

Now Boaz said to her at mealtime, "Come here, and eat of the bread, and dip your piece of bread in the vinegar." So she sat beside the reapers, and he passed parched grain to her; and she ate and was satisfied, and kept some back. And when she rose up to glean, Boaz commanded his young men, saying, "Let her glean even among the sheaves, and do not reproach her. Also let grain from the bundles fall purposely for her; leave it that she may glean, and do not rebuke her."

So she gleaned in the field until evening, and beat out what she had gleaned, and it was about an ephah of barley. Then she took it up and went into the city, and her mother-in-law saw what she had gleaned.

So she brought out and gave to her what she had kept back after she had been satisfied.

And her mother-in-law said to her, "Where have you gleaned today? And where did you work? Blessed be the one who took notice of you."

So she told her mother-in-law with whom she had worked, and said, "The man's name with whom I worked today is Boaz."

Then Naomi said to her daughter-in-law, "Blessed be he of the LORD, who has not forsaken His kindness to the living and the dead!" And Naomi said to her, "This man is a relation of ours, one of our close relatives."

Ruth the Moabitess said, "He also said to me, 'You shall stay close by my young men until they have finished all my harvest.'"

And Naomi said to Ruth her daughter-in-law, "It is good, my daughter, that you go out with his young women, and that people do not meet you in any other field." So she stayed close by the young women of Boaz, to glean until the end of barley harvest and wheat harvest; and she dwelt with her mother-in-law. (Ruth 2:1-22)

So Boaz took Ruth and she became his wife; and when he went in to her, the LORD gave her conception, and she bore a son. Then the women said to Naomi, "Blessed be the LORD, who has not left you this day without a close relative; and may his name be famous in Israel! And may he be to you a restorer of life and a nourisher of your old age; for your daughter-in-law, who loves you, who is better to you than seven sons, has borne him." Then Naomi took the child and laid him on her bosom, and became a nurse to him. Also the neighbor women gave him a name, saying, "There is a son born to Naomi." And they called his name Obed. He is the father of Jesse, the father of David.

Now this is the genealogy of Perez: Perez begot Hezron; Hezron begot Ram, and Ram begot Amminadab; Amminadab begot Nahshon, and Nahshon begot Salmon; Salmon begot Boaz, and Boaz begot Obed; Obed begot Jesse, and Jesse begot David. (Ruth 4:13-21)

This is one of the most profound stories about lasting impressions. Ruth decided to follow her mother-in-law Naomi back to her hometown after the death of her husband, Ruth's husband, and Naomi's other son. This was a saddening experience for Naomi to lose so many family members. Through her sorrow, she pressed forward with her daughter-in-law back to Judah.

Ruth was so faithful to Naomi that she believed in Naomi's God, the Great I Am–Lord of all. Well, Ruth was still a beautiful young lady and they both needed to eat, so Ruth went into the fields to glean grain behind the reapers as was customary for those who were not as affluent as others.

While Ruth was gleaning, she worked very hard gathering up grain so that she and Naomi could eat. She worked so hard and was such an interesting woman that Boaz noticed her. Boaz was impressed with her and asked who she was. He told his gleaners to leave extra for Ruth, and they did. He also instructed Ruth that she was to only glean in his field so that he could take care of her and ensure her safety during the harvest. Boaz was a gentleman to say the least…Boaz also, unknowingly to Ruth, until later, was a distant relative.

Ruth made a lasting impression on Boaz. He was willing to allow her to glean only in his fields, he gave her water and something to eat, left her some choice grain, and eventually (through a process) married her.

I believe that God orchestrated every move. What is God orchestrating for you in your life? Where does God have you gleaning that may eventually lead to increase for you and your family? Are you headed in a direction where you may get increased responsibility on your job or in the community? Is God enlarging your territory? Boaz married Ruth as her kinsman redeemer. Jesus is your kinsman redeemer and will cover you with His wings of protection and love just like Boaz did for Ruth. Jesus will love you as you do the work of the gospel to which you are called.

Jesus will notice your integrity, your hard work, your love for His people, your desire to feed them, and your humanity to give up your life for Him.

Are you destined to be around kings? I believe you are. Your gift will make room for you and bring you before great men. So, make a lasting impression through your faithfulness to God and to God alone.

Your thoughts:

In the space below, list additional reflections that you have in mind regarding God's purpose for your life right now. List what God has in mind for you over the next few years to see beyond the normal into the spiritual by your faithfulness to the things God has ordained you to accomplish.

17. Go Grow Your Field

Then Isaac sowed in that land, and reaped in the same year a hundredfold; and the LORD blessed him. The man began to prosper, and continued prospering until he became very prosperous; for he had possessions of flocks and possessions of herds and a great number of servants. So the Philistines envied him. Now the Philistines had stopped up all the wells which his father's servants had dug in the days of Abraham his father, and they had filled them with earth. (Genesis 26:12-15)

Your field can be vast depending on how you see it. I know a man from a small town in the south that grew up on a farm. His family were farmers and planted many types of crops as income. They knew that if they did not sow a crop, they would not reap a crop. They usually sowed corn, beans, potatoes, pecans, cucumbers, and other things. They also had cows and pigs, and they would sell the cows and pigs to earn a living.

When there was a good year and the weather was favorable, they had an excellent crop and would share food with their neighbors. During rough years, and there was not as much to go around, they still had enough to live on themselves.

I have heard many people say that you can tell where a person's heart is by his or her checkbook, where they spend their time, and what comes out of their mouth. Where they spend their money states where they plant seed that they expect to grow. If they are spending money on pleasures and not giving back to God, that seed will not produce a harvest. A person tithing and giving should expect an increased living. If they are spending their time with God and doing things that God requires, they can be assured of success according to His plan. Whatever they think will produce exactly what they say.

Isaac grew his field. He sowed in the exact land that God told him to sow in. Even though the Philistines envied him and tried to stop his progress, Isaac reaped a one hundred-fold harvest for His obedience.

Countless times, I have seen so many people sow and reap a harvest quickly. Other times, it takes a season of waiting on the harvest. Although the blessing is delayed, it is not denied. It is simple, sow your resources (time, talent, money, gifts) into the Kingdom and watch your field (ministry) grow. You will be like Jacob and have abundance above what you expect.

Your thoughts:

In the space below, make a list of where you spend your time, money, and God given gifts. Are you sowing into the right field? If so, great–congratulations! If not, how will you change and move in the direction that God has purposed for you?

18. Expect God to Show You the Way

For this cause everyone who is godly shall pray to You In a time when You may be found; surely in a flood of great waters they shall not come near him. You are my hiding place; You shall preserve me from trouble; You shall surround me with songs of deliverance.

I will instruct you and teach you in the way you should go; I will guide you with My eye. Do not be like the horse or like the mule, which have no understanding, which must be harnessed with bit and bridle, else they will not come near you.

Many sorrows shall be to the wicked; but he who trusts in the LORD, mercy shall surround him. Be glad in the LORD and rejoice, you righteous; and shout for joy, all you upright in heart! (Psalm 32:6-11)

I used this passage as exercise in church one Sunday morning. I believe my subject was about being led by God. Since this Sunday was dedicated to our youth, I asked the youth to come up to volunteer.

I had eye masks for them to put on. I asked a parent or guardian for each child to come up and assist them in putting on the covers. The kids were excited. There were smiles on their faces and some of them even giggled.

After the eye covers were secure, I told a story about being led by people versus being led by God or someone godly that they could trust (like a parent). The crux of the story was that you should only expect God to show you the right path in life, and that others may lead you astray.

I told them that they were to imagine that they were with a stranger and being lead around in life by ungodly things/people. I told them that they could end up in a place that was not desirable for them as believers if they followed the wrong crowd.

I asked them to agree to an experiment. They agreed. Upon agreement, I asked a guide to take them around. The guide came and walked them through the church sanctuary. The guide was directed to spin them around, and help them to navigate through the room. The giggles increased as they were lead around the room by the guides.

I instructed some of the guides to lightly run them into the benches, walk them up steps and down steps, and in between the benches. The guides were great, they followed directions well. At the end of this exercise, I asked the guides to sit them in a unique place in the church. And they did. While they were seated I continued with my story. I let them know that they should be careful who they hung out with and who led them in life. That they may end up in different places than expected.

At that time, I asked them to take off their masks and look around. They did...to their amazement, they were led to sit places that they had not expected. They were sitting next to strangers and did not know how they got there (the spinning around helped). They learned a valuable lesson. Expect God to show you the way. He will lead you…you can trust Him.

Your thoughts:

Who are your leaders? List at least 5. Are they leading you toward Christ or away from Christ? Document this on your paper.

19. Now Unto Him Who is Able

For this reason I bow my knees to the Father of our Lord Jesus Christ, from whom the whole family in heaven and earth is named, that He would grant you, according to the riches of His glory, to be strengthened with might through His Spirit in the inner man, that Christ may dwell in your hearts through faith; that you, being rooted and grounded in love, may be able to comprehend with all the saints what is the width and length and depth and height—to know the love of Christ which passes knowledge; that you may be filled with all the fullness of God.

Now to Him who is able to do exceedingly abundantly above all that we ask or think, according to the power that works in us, to Him be glory in the church by Christ Jesus to all generations, forever and ever. Amen. (Ephesians 3:14-20)

Where does ability reside? Some might say that their ability resides in their own strength, mind, or in their talents. That might be a fact, but really, our ability resides in God. He is the One who gives us our ability to do anything.

Have you ever watched a little kid try to do something like open up a well-secured package or reach a door handle that is too high for them? They will try and try to open up the package in so many different ways. They may even step on the package, put it into their mouths to try to open it, or some will

103

throw it on to the floor or hit it on the wall before giving up. In opening a cupboard door that is too high for them, they may try to jump up to the door to reach the handle or crawl onto a table or a chair to reach it.

In any case, the kids will try and try using all of their might and strength to solve the problem of opening up the package or door. As an adult, I have watched kids try and try again. I am always amazed how creative they are and how they may develop new strategies and techniques in getting the problem solved. When the problem seems too surmountable, the kid will ask for help.

We are that way, too. Some of us will try to do things ourselves without asking God for help. Have you ever watched an adult try to figure out a problem without asking God? I have done it countless times. It never occurred to me that in God's eyes I looked like that child who thought he/she had the solution for solving the problem him/herself.

I found over the years that the solution to my problem or challenge was right inside of me all the time; it is called ask, seek, and knock. God always has the solution and answers we need. Always. The quicker we realize how awesome our God is, the quicker we will get the results He provides.

God wants us to have the best of everything. He wants us to be successful and to have Him. As we seek His ways, plan, wisdom, love, and grace…please know that God has already provided everything you need in Him.

Your thoughts:

In the space below, list additional reflections that you have in mind regarding God's desire for you. What will He do for you that you have been longing for?

20. Cadence of the Anointing

But you have an anointing from the Holy One, and you know all things. I have not written to you because you do not know the truth, but because you know it, and that no lie is of the truth. (1 John 2:20)

But the anointing which you have received from Him abides in you, and you do not need that anyone teach you; but as the same anointing teaches you concerning all things, and is true, and is not a lie, and just as it has taught you, you will abide in Him. (1 John 2:27)

I used to play in several bands when I was younger (concert band, marching band and jazz band). I was younger. (Lol) Anyway in each band we always had a conductor, director, or band leader. The band director always selected the songs we were to play (he sometimes took our input), places we were to play, and when we were to play.

It was our duty to play for the football games, special events, and school pep rallies. I had a great time playing. I never knew all the work that went on behind the scenes, nor did I have an appreciation for what the band director went through to get every instrument in place, the songs right, and the students in alignment with his vision. We would sometimes compete in band competitions to place in the city, state, and nation. Practice was necessary for us to be good at it.

There was a need for us to know how to read music, know the beat of the music, and to play in appropriate times and intensity according to what was called for on the sheet music. Everyone knew their place and knew exactly when to play their instrument after hours of practice. I remember taking my clarinet different places with me so that I could practice placing my fingers correctly over the pads. After a while, I knew what to do. I knew where my fingers should be placed. It was simple. I could read the music, I could play on time, and keep up with the beat. I was also offered a solo role on occasion.

My mother would take me to competitions and practice and wait on me outside until I was done. She would make sure I was fed, got my homework done, and practiced more as needed.

Some people know exactly what I mean because they have also played an instrument before. Others know what I mean, because they have watched a conductor of a symphony, had friends or family who played, or they just like music.

With music, there is a rhythm, sequence of notes played, pauses, beat, sound, and movement. I used to rock to the beat when I would hear a song played whether it was familiar or not. I loved most any type of music from classical to gospel.

The Holy Spirit inside of us all has a rhythm or cadence. He is always connected to God and Jesus. They all are One and live in believers. He will set the tone for our lives when we surrender ourselves to His leading. He will select what we should do in life, our attitude for godly living, and teach us about our Heavenly Father in a more profound way than you could ever imagine.

We all carry the anointing in us. Jesus is the Anointed One. The anointing allows us to receive from God. God will teach us, lead, and help us in all things because we abide in cadence with Him. Allow the conductor to select the pace for your life, select the events where you will serve, and use you as His instrument of life. He will show you all things that pertain to life and godliness because you have the Holy One living within you.

The Holy Spirit guides and guards us as we abide in Him and walk in the truth of His Word. The walk of truth is in our ability to persevere in faithfulness and in the Word of God.

Your thoughts:

In the space below, list additional reflections that you have in mind regarding God's purpose for your life right now. List what God has in mind for you over the next few years to see beyond the normal and make a cadence in the spirit with Him.

21. Everyone Can Have It

The Lord is not slack concerning His promise, as some count slackness, but is longsuffering toward us, not willing that any should perish but that all should come to repentance. (2 Peter 3:9)

For this reason we also, since the day we heard it, do not cease to pray for you, and to ask that you may be filled with the knowledge of His will in all wisdom and spiritual understanding; that you may walk worthy of the Lord, fully pleasing Him, being fruitful in every good work and increasing in the knowledge of God; strengthened with all might, according to His glorious power, for all patience and longsuffering with joy; giving thanks to the Father who has qualified us to be partakers of the inheritance of the saints in the light. He has delivered us from the power of darkness and conveyed us into the kingdom of the Son of His love, in whom we have redemption through His blood, the forgiveness of sins. (Colossians 1:9-14)

And the Spirit and the bride say, "Come!" And let him who hears say, "Come!" And let him who thirsts come. Whoever desires, let him take the water of life freely. (Revelation 22:17)

We should always take the Word of God seriously. He wants all of us to receive the benefits of His blessing, which includes spiritual intellect. Jesus Christ Himself paid a dear price for us all to qualify to be partakers of His inheritance with all the saints. It is God's will for us to be delivered from the power of darkness and conveyed into His Kingdom. We are bought back by the blood of Jesus. We have forgiveness of sins though Jesus.

I know a gentleman who loves to talk about the farm that his father owned. When he was young, he had to work on the farm and help with the livestock. His father had paid the price for the land when he was very young. He purchased the land for him and his wife to enjoy. He also had in mind that his children could benefit from the land as well when they matured. The father worked the land for many years before he passed away. Although he was gone, he had made provisions to leave his land and possessions to his children. They now own the land and use it commercially for growing timber.

Jesus did a similar thing for us. He paid the price for us to inherit eternal life with him. This eternal life (salvation) includes complete healing and deliverance in this life. Jesus did not put limits on what could be done...all things are possible for us to be successful.

God wants us all to be filled with the knowledge of His will, have all spiritual understanding and spiritual intellect. He further wants us to be worthy of the Lord by being pleasing to Him in our actions, words, and living. As we desire God and meditate on His Word day and night, we will each be like a tree planted by steams of water where our leaves do not wither and we live in good soil. Everything we do will prosper.

God wants us to live this life with Him as Lord. It is not God's desire for anyone to perish; He wants us all to have everlasting life. The Spirit and the bride say come. Whoever desires let him partake of the water of life freely. Everyone can have it.

Your thoughts:

In the space below, list additional reflections that you have in mind regarding God's purpose for your life right now. List scripture to let you know that you have what God says you can have in this life.

NOTES

114

In conclusion:

So, how did it go for you? Did you learn how God equipped you with spiritual intellect to serve His Kingdom? Now, we have confirmed that every believer has the intellect, power, and authority to make things happen for the Kingdom of God. Through prompt obedience, careful study of the Word, continual prayer, and exercising Kingdom rights–there are so many successes that can come to fruition. Like I said in the introduction, there is nothing impossible with God. There is nothing too hard for Him.

I trust you have enjoyed reading these pages and prayerfully completing the exercises at the end of each section, as much as I enjoyed listening to God while writing them. Continue to pray that God will open your eyes to see how to be more impactful for His Kingdom through reading this Spiritual Quick Book™. Now, go; affect God's Kingdom with your spiritual intellect!!

Spiritual Intellect includes:

S – See Beyond the Normal
P – Place Your Thoughts in the Original
I – Intellect Goes Beyond What the Eye Can See
R – Realms of Intellect
I – Intentional Rotation
T – The Thoughts of God
U – Unfettered Access
A – Ambassadorship Versus Citizenship
L – Lessons from Successful Pioneers

I – Irrefutable Future
N – Next Realm, Please
T – Tell it from the Valley
E – Engineered to be Successful
L – Letting Go of Distorted Ideas
L – Living Out Your Dream
I – Impressions are Lasting
G – Go Grow Your Field
E – Expect God to Show You the Way
N – Now Unto Him Who is Able
C – Cadence of the Anointing
E – Everyone Can Have It

Live in your Kingdom spiritual authority as a powerful person in Christ, bear good fruit, and make things happen in the mighty Name of Jesus our Lord!

BIBLIOGRAPHY

New American Standard Bible, Updated Edition, 1995.

Exhaustive Concordance of the Bible. (Lahabra, CA: The Lockman Foundation -- Foundation Publications, Inc. Anaheim, CA); 1981, 1998.

The Spirit Filled Bible (NKJV). (Nelson Publishing), 2002.

Merriam-Webster's Collegiate Dictionary. (Merriam-Webster); 10th Edition, 1998.

Munroe, Dr. Myles (1954-), president and founder of Bahamas Faith Ministries International.

www.BibleGateway.com

117

NOTES

About the Author

Dr. Amanda H. Goodson

Goodson is a native of Decatur, Alabama and currently resides in Tucson, Arizona where God has entrusted her to serve as Pastor of Trinity Temple Christian Methodist Episcopal Church. She also plans and facilitates seminars, workshops, and retreats for the CME church.

She is President and on the board of Directors for Never the Same Ministries (NTS), a God inspired, Tucson based, Kingdom ministry dedicated to serve as a vessel through which people are provided tools and resources to develop a more spiritually mature and improved relationship with God through Christ. The NTS God ordered mission is to provide biblically based instruction, tools and coaching for people within the community through planning and deployment of conferences and events across the United States.

God has gifted Goodson to be a Spirit led preacher, teacher, trainer and coach for churches, agencies and non-profit organizations. Goodson connects with her audiences by sharing the Word of God through real-life experiences. She gives God glory as He allows her to inspire others to learn more about being a Spirit led Christian in the world today.

God has blessed her with an enthusiastic, energized and interactive method.

Goodson is fully committed to the Lord and knows that she has a blessed Spirit led life. Her purpose is the fill the earth with knowledge of God's glory by serving the Lord boldly through her ministry; bringing others closer to Christ and introducing Christ to those who have not accepted Him as their personal savior. God's Word is her authority. Goodson believes that God's presence and power is Almighty and worthy to be praised. Further, she knows that God will make great things happen through His people.

Amanda has a Bachelor's of Science in Electrical Engineering from Tuskegee University, a Master's of Science in Management from Florida Institute of Technology, and a Doctor of Ministry from United Theological Seminary specializing in church administration.

She is married to a godly man and has one a son.

As a kingdom citizen, she is fully submitted to the will of God. Her prayer is to be active in sharing her faith, to make her thoughts agreeable to the will of God, and to have the mind of Christ. The Word of God is the final authority in her life.

For a complete listing of CDs, DVDs, and books by Dr. Amanda Goodson, or to participate in a ministry conference, book a conference, speaking event or training, please email or visit the following web site:

NTSMinistries@aol.com

or visit

ntsministries.org

Books by Dr. Amanda Goodson

Spiritual Quickbooks ™
Kingdom Character
Spiritual Authority
Carmel Voices
The Power to Make an Impact
Powerful People Follow Christ
Step out in Faith
Going Higher, Declarations for Kids
On the Rise

Leadership Minibooks ™
The Authority of a Leader
Powerful People Lead

Photo by Martha Lochert